CELEBRITY BIOS

Will Smith

by
Kristin McCracken

HIGH
interest
books

Children's Press
A Division of Grolier Publishing
New York / London / Hong Kong / Sydney
Danbury, Connecticut

To Jennifer, Kristine, Katie, Ellen, Jenny, and Amy

Photo Credits: Cover, p. 29 © Pacha/Corbis; p. 4 © Fitzroy Barrett/Globe Photos Inc.; p. 6 © Tom Rodriguez/Globe Photos Inc.; p. 10 © Ronnie Wright/Corbis; p. 12 © Dave G. Morgan/Alpha/Globe Photos; pp. 15, 17 © Sin/David Anderson/Corbis; pp.19, 22, 26, 35, 37 © Everett Collection; p. 20 © Alan Levenson/Corbis; p. 25 © Stephanie Jennings/Corbis; p. 32 © Lisa Rose/Globe Photos.

Visit Children's Press on the Internet at:
http://publishing.grolier.com

Library of Congress Cataloging-in-Publication Data

McCracken, Kristin.
   Will Smith / by Kristin McCracken.
      p. cm.–(Celebrity bios)
   Includes bibliographical references and index.
   Summary: Discusses the personal life and career of the rap musician and actor, Will Smith.
   ISBN 0-516-23327-0 (lib.bdg.) – ISBN 0-516-23527-3 (pbk.)
   1. Smith, Will, 1968–Juvenile literature. 2. Actors–United States–Biography–Juvenile literature. 3. Rap musicians–United States–Biography–Juvenile literature. [1. Smith, Will, 1968- 2. Actors and actresses. 3. Musicians. 4. Rap (Music) 5. Afro-Americans–Biography.] I. Title. II. Celebrity bios (Children's Press)

PN2287.S612M39 2000
791.43'028'092–dc21
[B]
                                                                99-058248

CONTENTS

1 A Star is Born   5
2 Making Music   13
3 Life on the Small Screen   21
4 Silver-Screen Success   27
   Timeline   40
   Fact Sheet   42
   New Words   43
   For Further Reading   45
   Resources   46
   Index   47
   About the Author   48

CHAPTER ONE

A Star Is Born

"I'm headed somewhere greater. I just don't know what it is yet." — Will Smith in *Teen*

Will Smith is one of today's biggest film and music stars. He's known as one of the hardest-working people in show business. Yet Will also is a caring husband and father, as well as a role model. With his dimples, warm smile, and what he calls his "jug ears," Will has charmed audiences all over the world. Whether he's rapping on MTV or fighting aliens on the big screen, Will Smith does everything with his own brand of style and humor.

Will Smith with his mother, Caroline

THE EARLY YEARS

Willard C. ("Will") Smith, Jr., was born in Philadelphia, Pennsylvania, on September 25, 1968. Will was the first son of Willard and Caroline Smith. The Smith family also includes an older sister named Pamela and two younger twins, Harry and Ellen.

The Smiths were strict but loving middle-class parents. They believed hard work was the way to success. The Smiths also believed very strongly in the importance of learning. Will often has said that his parents helped to make him the successful person that he is today. "The only people that I ever idolized are my parents," Will told *Biography* magazine.

Will's parents divorced when he was thirteen. Will and his siblings went to live with their mother. Will's father, however, continued to play a big part in his young son's life.

Did you know?

Will's favorite books when he was a toddler were written by Dr. Seuss. Says Will, "If you listen to them a certain way, books like *Green Eggs and Ham* and *Hop on Pop* sound a lot like hip-hop music."

In Philadelphia, Will attended a Catholic school, called Our Lady of Lourdes, from kindergarten to 8th grade. Later, he went to Overbrook High School. Will's favorite subjects were math, science, and English. He began to experiment with writing poetry. But something else that Will liked to do was make people laugh. He realized that he could crack up his classmates with a wacky face or a silly joke. Will's teachers also found him funny. One teacher even called Will "Prince Charming," because he made up such good excuses for not turning in his homework.

Yet Will wasn't able to charm everyone. One teacher complained to

Did you know?

In a national survey of teenage girls, Will Smith beat out Jim Carrey and Tom Cruise to win most admired star.

Will's mother that he wasn't working hard enough. "I was the fun student who had trouble paying attention," Will admitted to *Teen*. "I was a B student who should've been getting As—a classic underachiever." Will's parents stepped in and turned him around. Soon, Will became one of the best science students at Overbrook High. In his high school yearbook, Will said that he wanted to become an engineer.

In 1986, when Will was a high school senior, he found out that he'd won a scholarship to the Milwaukee School of Engineering. He turned it down. By that time, Will realized that his goals had changed. Music had become his true ambition in life.

WILL THE MUSICIAN

In 1979, eleven-year-old Will heard his first rap song on the radio. The song was "Rapper's Delight" by a band called the Sugar Hill Gang. Will instantly was hooked. He thought the lyrics

Will as the Fresh Prince and Jeff Townes, or DJ Jazzy Jeff

sounded like a kind of poetry. He also liked the fact that rap lyrics sometimes were funny.

In 1985, when Will was sixteen, he met his future rap partner Jeff Townes. Townes, who called himself DJ Jazzy Jeff, was dee-jaying at a local rap party in south Philadelphia. Within weeks, Will and Jeff were writing and recording songs together.

DJ Jazzy Jeff already had a great stage name. Will needed to find one that was just as snappy. Will decided to use part of his nickname from school. He added a popular term from the rap scene that meant "cool, hip, the best."

The Fresh Prince was born.

CHAPTER TWO

Making Music

"We want to bring rap out of the ghetto. We're presenting problems that relate to everybody." —The Fresh Prince in *People*

Early in 1986, Will and Jeff decided they had enough songs to make an album. The pair took their material to the local Word Up record label. Record producer Dana Goodman immediately signed the two to a record contract.

Before Will had even finished high school, the first album by DJ Jazzy Jeff and the Fresh Prince was released. The record, *Rock the House*, and the single, "Girls Ain't Nothing But Trouble," came out in 1987. Not only was the single a hit in Philadelphia, it became an anthem for teenage boys everywhere.

The duo's sound was different from most rap records that were being released. Their music was more fun and less serious. They also did not curse in their songs or rap about violence, as did a lot of rappers. Will told *Biography* magazine, "I would never do anything that my mother couldn't turn on her radio and listen to. I would never do anything to offend my family."

Rock the House sold 600,000 copies, enough to qualify as a gold record. Will was just seventeen years old. Suddenly, he and DJ Jazzy Jeff were an overnight, international success.

THE NEXT STEP

Early in 1988, Will and Jeff made another record called *He's the DJ, I'm the Rapper.* It was hip-hop's first double album. The record went multiplatinum, selling more than two and a half million copies.

Will's rapping skills led to the huge success of the album *He's the DJ, I'm the Rapper.*

The first single was called "Parents Just Don't Understand." The song was about teens' struggles with their parents. The hilarious music video helped to land the song in the number twelve spot on the pop music chart. Once again, Will and Jeff helped prove that hip-hop was not just for African-Americans, but for people of all races. This was important to Will. "We wanted to write about something everybody could relate to," Will recalled to *People*. "We make it universal. My point of view isn't limited. It's very broad. It's more than the black experience."

LEARNING A LESSON

Jeff and Will knew they had to keep their fans happy. They were an act that had rarely performed live since they became famous. They wanted to give their fans a chance to see them in person. In 1988, DJ Jazzy Jeff and the Fresh Prince went on a tour of the United States. They opened for Run DMC, another popular rap band.

Before the tour, both Will and Jeff had been living with their parents. Suddenly, they were away from home, surrounded by fans, and earning

Will and Jeff were both very young when they became millionaires.

huge amounts of money. Will was just twenty years old, but he was already a millionaire. He wanted to live the life of a rich musician. While on tour, he ate at the fanciest restaurants. He bought expensive clothes and jewelry.

Will's outrageous spending habits didn't end when the tour finished. In the fall of 1988, Will came back to Philadelphia and bought a huge mansion. He had a basketball hoop installed—in the living room! He bought a pool table and a hot tub. He also bought six luxury cars.

Will was rich, but he also had no idea how to handle his money. Before long, he received a letter from the United States government. It said that he owed more than one million dollars in taxes! Suddenly, Will had six cars and couldn't afford to buy gas.

To pay his huge tax bill, Will had to sell the mansion and his cars. He moved back home with his mother. Will explained to *People* what happened at that time in his life: "Money disappears a lot faster than it comes in, no matter how much you make. Being able to buy anything you want makes you a little crazy."

AWARD-WINNER

Will may have been having problems with money, but his music career was going well. DJ Jazzy Jeff and the Fresh Prince won several awards in 1988. At the American Music Awards, "He's the DJ, I'm the Rapper" was named Best Rap Single. Soon after, they won a Grammy Award for Best

Rap Performance for "Parents Just Don't Understand." It was the first year ever that a Grammy was given out in a rap category. DJ Jazzy Jeff and the Fresh Prince had proven that rap could not be ignored by the music industry.

CHAPTER THREE

Life on the Small Screen

"It's a whole different thing being an actor. A rapper is about being completely true to yourself. Being an actor is about changing who you are." — Will in *Newsday*

In 1989, Will was visiting friends in California. In Los Angeles, he ran into Benny Medina, a young African-American record executive. Medina told Will about an idea he had for a television show. It would be a sitcom about a young black man from Philadelphia who comes to live with relatives in Bel Air, California. Medina wanted Will Smith to be the show's star.

"The Fresh Prince of Bel-Air" was an immediate hit when it debuted on NBC.

Although Will had never acted before, he decided to take the part. Once Will signed on, the show got its name—"The Fresh Prince of Bel-Air." Will was twenty-one years old when he moved to Los Angeles to begin working on the show. He was very nervous about his acting abilities. He was so determined to learn his lines that he ended up memorizing the entire script. Sometimes he would even move his mouth to the other actors' lines!

"The Fresh Prince of Bel-Air" went on the air in September 1990. The show was an instant hit. People tuned in to see an African-American teenager who was smart, funny, cool, and who loved hip-hop. Will had a natural charm that appealed to television audiences of all races and backgrounds. He was pleased to be part of a show that portrayed African-Americans in a positive way. Will explained to *Biography*, "What I'm happy about is that I can be a role model and give people something to think about."

MUSIC AND MORE

Will was a TV star, but he also wanted to continue making music. In early 1991, Will arranged for his old friend and rap partner Jeff Townes (DJ Jazzy Jeff) to join the cast of "The Fresh Prince of Bel-Air." Townes appeared as a character named

"Jazz." The two worked on the show during the day and on a new album called *Homebase* at night.

In July 1991, the single "Summertime" was released. It was one of the duo's biggest hits. That same year, DJ Jazzy Jeff and the Fresh Prince won their second Grammy award, for Best Rap Performance by a Duo or Group. "Summertime" earned an American Music Award for Best Rap Single.

The spring of 1992 brought some awards for Will's acting. Will was honored with a Golden Globe nomination for Best Performance by an Actor in a Television Series. He also received an NAACP Image Award for Best Comedy Series for "The Fresh Prince of Bel-Air."

Not only was Will's professional life going well, his personal life was, too. In May 1992,

Did you know?

The two things that Will hates the most are bad grammar and smoking.

Will and his first wife, Sheree Zampino, met on the set of her television show.

Will married Sheree Zampino, a woman he had met while visiting the set of the TV show "A Different World."

CHAPTER FOUR

Silver-Screen Success

*"The bottom line with me is fun. I enjoy life;
I enjoy people. And people—black, white,
Asian, or alien—enjoy that energy."*
—Will in *Biography* magazine

It was the summer of 1992 and Will had finished
taping the second season of "The Fresh Prince of
Bel-Air." The show's success gave Will the chance
to act on the big screen. First, he was cast as Tea
Cake Walters in a big-budget comedy with Whoopi
Goldberg called *Made in America*. The movie gave
Will good experience, but he wanted to take on
more serious roles. He found what he was looking

for in his second movie of the summer, *Six Degrees of Separation.*

The film, which was based on a Broadway play, took a serious look at racism in America. Will played David Hampton, a young black man who tricks his way into a wealthy white family by pretending to be someone he's not. In *Six Degrees of Separation,* Will was able to prove to himself and to the critics that he could act.

FATHERHOOD

The fall of 1992 was extremely busy for Will. He began taping the third season of "The Fresh Prince of Bel-Air." He and DJ Jazzy Jeff were busy recording another album. But for Will, the biggest thrill of all was becoming a father.

Will and Sheree's son, Willard C. Smith III, was born in November. They nicknamed him Trey. Will was determined to give his son the same strong love and support he had received from his own parents. "When the doctor handed

Will and his son Trey in matching outfits

[Trey] to me, I realized things were different now," Will recalled in *Premiere*. "I couldn't be a reckless young man anymore."

In 1993, the family bought a home in the Los Angeles suburb of Thousand Oaks. Will began work on the fourth season of the successful television show. But while Will's career seemed to be in great shape, things were falling apart at home. Will loved being a father, but his marriage to Zampino wasn't working. In early 1995, he and Zampino split up. They both agreed, however, to play a big part in Trey's upbringing.

FROM BAD TO GOOD

In 1995, Will teamed up with Martin Lawrence to make the action comedy *Bad Boys*. Lawrence was a popular African-American comedian who had his own TV show, "Martin."

Bad Boys became a huge hit with movie audiences. Will won a 1996 Blockbuster Entertainment Award for Best New Actor in an Action/Comedy. Suddenly, Will was being offered $5 million to star in his next film. He decided that his acting future would be in the movies, not on television. In 1995,

Will returned to tape the sixth, and final, season of "The Fresh Prince of Bel-Air."

A NEW LOVE

As Will's television career was ending, a new part of his life was just beginning. For several years, Will had known the actress Jada Pinkett. In 1990, Pinkett had tried out for the part of the Fresh Prince's girlfriend. Producers decided that she was too short, but Pinkett had gone on to have a successful career of her own.

In the fall of 1995, the two began spending more and more time together. They quickly realized that their relationship was more than just a close friendship. By the spring of 1996, Will and "Miss Jada," as he calls her, were an item.

FROM MOVIE STAR TO MEGASTAR

After the success of *Bad Boys*, Will had his pick of movie roles. He chose to play the part of a Marine fighter pilot in the science-fiction picture

Jada and Will in 1996

Independence Day. When he began filming in the summer of 1995, Will had no idea that the movie would make him a household name.

Independence Day, or *ID4*, as it came to be

known, exploded onto movie screens over the 1996 July 4th holiday. Within one week, the movie had made $100 million—$30 million more than it had cost to make. *ID4* set box-office records worldwide. The one name on everyone's lips that summer was Will Smith.

WILL VS. MORE ALIENS

The following year, Will Smith followed up with another science-fiction movie, *Men in Black*. *Men in Black*, or *MiB*, again saw Will saving the Earth from invading aliens. Will co-starred with Tommy Lee Jones as a wise-cracking government agent who fights creatures from outer space. The film made $51 million in its opening over the July 4th weekend. It broke the record *ID4* had set the year before.

Will Smith came to be known as the king of the July 4th movie. "It's just my job to save the world every summer," he joked in *Biography*.

Will also wrote and recorded two songs for the

MiB soundtrack. Will's title song from the movie, "*Men in Black*," was heard on radio stations all summer long. The song helped Will to win his third Grammy, for Best Solo Rap Performance in 1998. He also received an MTV Movie Award for Best Movie Song for "*Men in Black*."

BACK IN STYLE

In December 1997, Will released his first solo album, *Big Willie Style*. This time, Will used his own name instead of Fresh Prince. Not one to forget his old friends, Will asked Jeff Townes to produce three of the songs on the record. The album included the "*Men in Black*" theme song, as well as two more smash singles: "Gettin' Jiggy Wit It" and "Just the Two of Us." *Big Willie Style* quickly went multiplatinum, selling more than six million copies. Will accepted MTV's Best Male Video award for "Just the Two of Us" with his co-star and son, Trey. "Gettin' Jiggy Wit It" won an MTV Best Rap Video award and a Grammy for

Will not only acted in *Men In Black*, he contributed two songs to the movie's soundtrack.

Best Rap Solo.

Will decided to end his incredibly successful year with a bang. On New Year's Eve in 1997, Will Smith and Jada Pinkett were married. Soon after their honeymoon in Miami, the young couple had another announcement. They were expecting their first child. In the summer of 1998, Jada gave birth to a son, Jaden Christopher Syre Smith.

That summer also was the first time in three years that Will did not have a blockbuster release. Will's sixth movie, *Enemy of the State*, came out in November 1998. The thriller, which also starred Gene Hackman, made a respectable $100 million. It also earned Will an MTV nomination for Best Male Performance. "One thing I've learned is that the right concept for my career is balance," Will explained to *Teen People*. "I did *Enemy of the State* . . . just so people don't forget I can act."

WILD WILD WILL

In the fall of 1998, Will returned to his action comedy roots. He was back on a movie set with *Men in Black* director Barry Sonnenfeld. They were making a film remake of a 1960s TV show

Will as agent James West in *Wild Wild West*

called "The Wild, Wild West." Will was cast as James West, a federal agent who helps to save the wild west from a villain.

As were many of Will's blockbuster movies, *Wild Wild West* was released over the July 4th weekend. Unfortunately, the movie opened to poor reviews from critics. *Wild Wild West* was not a complete failure, but audiences did not flock to movie theaters as they had for Will's other films.

Will was disappointed that people didn't like his latest picture. Still, he wasn't surprised, as he explained in an interview with *E!Online:* "I just feel a sense that some people think, 'He's a little high on this *Wild Wild West* horse, so he needs to get knocked down a little bit.'"

WHAT'S NEXT?

The summer of 1999 saw Will Smith back in the recording studio. He teamed up again with Jeff Townes to write songs for the album *Willenium,* released in November of that year. Will also has started a new record label. He's developing two movies with his film production company. One project is based on the life of boxer Muhammed

Ali. The other movie will be a remake of the film *A Star is Born*.

Will also will do the voice of a character in the animated film *Osmosis Jones*, due out in 2001. His love of golf helped him make the decision to play a caddy in *The Legend of Bagger Vance*, co-starring Matt Damon. He will star alongside wife Jada Pinkett in a movie that they wrote together called *Love for Sale*. He's also doing another film project, *The Mark*, about a battle at the end of the millenium. In the works are sequels to two of Will's most successful films, *Men in Black* and *Bad Boys*.

With the love of his family and his success as a television, film, and music star, is there anything that Will Smith can't do? Will doesn't think so. "I have no idea what my limits are," he told *People*. "I believe that if I set my mind to it, I would be the next President of the United States."

TIMELINE

1968 • Will Smith is born on September 25.

1986 • Will wins a scholarship to the Milwaukee School of Engineering but decides not to attend.
• Will and rap partner Jeff Townes get a record contract and name themselves DJ Jazzy Jeff and the Fresh Prince.

1987 • The record *Rock the House* is released.

1988 • *He's the DJ, I'm the Rapper* is released.
• DJ Jazzy Jeff and the Fresh Prince win a Grammy award for Best Rap Performance and an American Music Award for Best Rap Single.

1989 • "Parents Just Don't Understand" wins an MTV Video Music Award for Best Rap Video.
• The record *And in This Corner* is released.

1990 • "The Fresh Prince of Bel-Air" premieres.

1991 • The album *Homebase* is released.
• DJ Jazzy Jeff and the Fresh Prince win a Grammy for Best Rap Performance.
• Will appears as the Fresh Prince on an episode of the TV show "Blossom."

1992 • Will marries Sheree Zampino.
• Son Willard C. Smith III ("Trey") is born in November.
• Will is nominated for a Golden Globe award for "The Fresh Prince of Bel-Air."
• Will's first film, *Where the Day Takes You*, is released.

1993	• The movies *Made in America* and *Six Degrees of Separation* are released. • *Code Red* is in record stores.
1994	• Will hosts the MTV Movie Awards.
1995	• The blockbuster *Bad Boys* is released. • Will divorces Sheree Zampino.
1996	• *Independence Day* is released on July 4. • The last episode of "The Fresh Prince of Bel-Air" airs.
1997	• *Men in Black* comes out on July 4. • The soundtrack to *Men in Black* is released. • *Big Willie Style* is in record stores. • Will marries Jada Pinkett. • Will wins an MTV Music Award for Best Video from a Film for *"Men in Black."*
1998	• DJ Jazzy Jeff and the Fresh Prince's *Greatest Hits* is released. • Will and Jada's son Jaden is born. • *Enemy of the State* is released. • Will wins a Grammy for Best Rap Solo Performance for *"Men in Black."* • "Gettin' Jiggy Wit It" wins an MTV Video Music Award for Best Rap Video. • "Just the Two of Us" wins an MTV Video Music Award for Best Male Video. • Will is chosen as one of the Fifty Most Beautiful People by *People* magazine.
1999	• *Wild Wild West* is released. • The album *Willenium* is released. • Will wins MTV's Best Male Video Award for "Miami."

FACT SHEET

Name	Willard C. Smith, Jr.
Nicknames	Will, Fresh Prince
Born	September 25, 1968
Birthplace	Philadelphia, Pennsylvania
Parents	Will, Sr. and Caroline, divorced
Siblings	Pamela (older), twins Harry and Ellen (younger)
Wife	Jada Pinkett Smith
Children	Willard C. Smith, III (Trey), Jaden Christopher Syre Smith
Sign	Libra
Hair	Brown
Height	6' 2"
Eyes	Brown
Weight	200 pounds
Pets	Four Rottweiler dogs (two were a gift from Jay Leno)
Cars	Range Rover, Chevy Suburban

Favorites

Music	Anything LOUD
Hobbies	Golf, Chess
Team	Philadelphia 76ers (basketball)

NEW WORDS

audition a try-out performance for a role in a movie or TV show

chart a listing that ranks music sales

critic someone who gives his or her opinion of a movie, TV show, or play

director the person in charge of creating a movie, play, or TV show

duo two people

gold record certificate awarded to a record that sells half a million (500,000) copies

Grammy award an award given in recognition of musical achievement

hip-hop music that features breaks, multiple "samples" of songs, and often rapping

multiplatinum record certificate awarded to a record that sells more than two million copies

nomination selection of someone for an award

pop relating to popular music, as in "pop chart"

producer the person who supervises the production of an album, a film, or a television program

rap a form of rhythmic speaking in rhyme, often spoken over a hip-hop beat

record label a company that produces and sells records

recording studio place where music is recorded and produced

season a specific period of the year when a television series airs

science fiction kind of story that deals with scientific subjects or alien beings

sequel follow-up to a movie

sitcom television comedy show, usually half an hour in length

solo a song sung only by one person

soundtrack the music recorded for a movie

FOR FURTHER READING

Berenson, Jan. *Will Power! A Biography of Will Smith.* New York: Pocket Books, 1997.

Nickson, Chris. *Will Smith.* New York: St. Martin's Press, 1999.

Rodriguez, K.S. *Will Smith: From Fresh Prince to King of Cool.* New York: HarperCollins Juvenile Books, 1998.

RESOURCES

The Official *Men in Black* Web Site
www.meninblack.com
Includes behind-the-scenes information and footage about the making of the movie. Also includes a photo gallery and links to MiB merchandise.

The Official Will Smith Web Site
www.willsmith.net
Everything you need to know about Will's music, television, and film work. Includes a photo gallery and updates on the latest Will Smith news. Hosts a chat room for fans and provides links to other Will Smith Web sites.

Will Smith's IMDB Page
http://us.imdb.com/Name?Smith,+Will
This Internet Movie Database page has complete information on all of Will's movies and television appearances, as well as biographical material.

INDEX

A

Ali, Muhammed, 39
American Music Awards, 18, 24

B

Bad Boys, 30, 31, 39
Big Willie Style, 34
Blockbuster Entertainment Award, 30

D

"Different World, A," 25
DJ Jazzy Jeff, 11, 13, 14, 16, 18, 19, 23, 24, 28

E

Enemy of the State, 36

F

Fresh Prince, 11, 13, 16, 18, 24, 31, 34
"Fresh Prince of Bel-Air, The," 22–24, 27, 28, 31

G

"Gettin' Jiggy Wit It," 34

"Girls Ain't Nothing But Trouble," 13
gold record, 14
Golden Globe nomination, 24
Grammy Award, 18, 19, 24, 34

H

He's the DJ, I'm the Rapper, 18
hip-hop, 14,16, 23
Homebase, 24

I

Independence Day, 32, 33

L

Lawrence, Martin, 30
Legend of Bagger Vance, The, 39
Los Angeles, 22, 30
Love for Sale, 39

M

Made in America, 27
Mark, The, 39
Men in Black, 33, 34, 36, 39

Milwaukee School of
      Engineering 9,
MTV Movie Awards, 34, 36
MTV Music Awards, 34
multiplatinum record, 14, 34

N
NAACP Image Award, 24

O
Osmosis Jones, 39
Our Lady of Lourdes, 8
Overbrook High School, 8, 9

P
"Parents Just Don't
      Understand,"15, 19
Philadelphia, 6, 8,11, 14,17, 21
Pinkett, Jada, 31, 35, 36
poetry, 8,11

R
rap, 5, 9, 11, 14, 16, 19
Rock the House, 13, 14
Run DMC, 16

S
sequel, 39
Six Degrees of Separation, 28
Smith, Caroline, 6, 7
Smith, Jaden, 36
Smith, Trey, 28, 29, 30
Sr. Smith, Willard C., 6, 7
solo, 34, 35
soundtrack, 34
Sugar Hill Gang, 9

T
tour, 16, 17
Townes, Jeff, 11, 13, 14, 16,
      18, 19, 23, 24, 28, 34, 38

W
Wild Wild West, 38
Willenium, 38
Word Up record label, 13

Z
Zampino, Sheree, 25, 28, 30

ABOUT THE AUTHOR

Kristin McCracken is an educator and writer living in New York City. Her favorite activities include seeing movies, plays, and the occasional star on the street.